Witty Women

Ariel Books

Andrews and McMeel
Kansas City

Witty Women

WISE,
WICKED, & WONDERFUL
WORDS

ISBN: 0–8362–3067–1

Library of Congress Catalog Card Number: 93–73357

Contents

Introduction

What makes us laugh? What we know—
the familiar—turned on its head and jabbed
with a fork. For centuries, what women have
known best is domestic life and all it entails—
home, family, marriage, sex. From this fertile
ground has sprung some of the wittiest quotes in
this collection. No topic is sacred to the woman
who knows how to turn a phrase.

But don't think women left their sense of
humor at home when they ventured into the

public arena. As women have gained confidence
in their newly acquired roles in politics and the
workplace, their wit has kept pace, and they have
learned how to jab their forks a little deeper.

At home or at work, the wit of women
helps us keep everything in perspective. But perhaps the best quote of all, the one to remember, is
one from actress Ethel Barrymore: "You grow up
the day you have your first real laugh—at yourself." Or if you're of a more cynical frame of
mind, you might want to heed comedian Lily
Tomlin and remember: "We're all in this alone."

LIFE
LESSONS

If I had to live my life again I'd make all the same mistakes—only sooner.

—Tallulah Bankhead

If you're going to be able to look back on something and laugh about it, you might as well laugh about it now.

—Marie Osmond

I have come to the conclusion, after many years of sometimes sad experience, that you cannot come to any conclusion at all.

—Vita Sackville-West

Maybe being oneself is always an acquired taste.

—Patricia Hampl

Be bold in what you stand for and careful what you fall for.

—Ruth Boorstin

I have a simple philosophy. Fill what's empty. Empty what's full. And scratch where it itches.

—Alice Roosevelt Longworth

We're all in this alone.

—Lily Tomlin

Expecting life to treat you well because you are a good person is like expecting an angry bull not to charge because you are a vegetarian.

—Shari R. Barr

Never mistake knowledge for wisdom. One helps you make a living; the other helps you make a life.

—Sandra Carey

Those who do not know how to weep with their whole heart don't know how to laugh either.

—Golda Meir

I've been rich and I've been poor; rich is better.

—Sophie Tucker

When fate's got it in for you there's no limit to what you may have to put up with.

—Georgette Heyer

Never eat more than you can lift.

—Miss Piggy

Regret is an appalling waste of energy; you can't build on it; it's only good for wallowing in.

—Katherine Mansfield

You cannot shake hands with a clenched fist.
—Indira Gandhi

Never lend your car to anyone to whom you have given birth.
—Erma Bombeck

Off-the-rack solutions, like bargain basement dresses, never fit anyone.
—Françoise Giroud

DOMESTIC
LIFE

I can't mate in captivity.

—Gloria Steinem

Love, the quest; marriage, the conquest;
divorce, the inquest.

—Helen Rowland

Scratch a lover and find a foe.

—Dorothy Parker

I buried a lot of ironing in the backyard.
—Phyllis Diller

The only thing that seems eternal and natural
in motherhood is ambivalence.
—Jane Lazarre

The real menace in dealing with a five-year-old is that in no time at all you begin to sound like a five-year-old.

—Jean Kerr

I hate housework! You make the beds, you do the dishes—and six months later you have to start all over again.

—Joan Rivers

My idea of superwoman is someone who scrubs her own floors.

—Bette Midler

A successful parent is one who raises a child who grows up and is able to pay for her or his own psychoanalysis.

—Nora Ephron

Love never dies of starvation, but often of indigestion.

—Ninon de l'Enclos

It's matrimonial suicide to be jealous when you have a really good reason.

—Clare Boothe Luce

Oh, don't worry about Alan . . . Alan will always land on somebody's feet.

> —Dorothy Parker,
> on her divorce from Alan Campbell

I know what I wish Ralph Nader would investigate next. Marriage. It's not safe—it's not safe at all.

> —Jean Kerr

Cleaning your house while the kids are still growing is like shoveling the walk before it stops snowing.

—Phyllis Diller

Marriage may have turned into a junk bond. But nothing is so romantic as a risk.

—Tracy Young

People are always asking couples whose marriage has endured at least a quarter of a century for their secret for success. Actually, it is no secret at all. I am a forgiving woman. Long ago, I forgave my husband for not being Paul Newman.

—Erma Bombeck

I do not refer to myself as a "housewife" for the reason that I did not marry a house.

—Wilma Scott Heide

Nobody knows what anyone's marriage is like except the two of them—and sometimes one of them doesn't know.

—Ann Landers

SEX

After we made love he took a piece of chalk and made an outline of my body.

—Joan Rivers

I wrote the story myself. It's all about a girl who lost her reputation but never missed it.

—Mae West

A youth with his first cigar makes himself sick; a youth with his first girl makes everybody sick.

—Mary Wilson Little

Woman's virtue is man's greatest invention.
—Cornelia Otis Skinner

Sex appeal is 50 percent what you've got and 50 percent what people think you've got.
—Sophia Loren

The only reason I would take up jogging is so that I could hear heavy breathing again.

—Erma Bombeck

Sex is never an emergency.

—Elaine Pierson

It's the good girls who keep the diaries; the bad girls never have the time.

—Tallulah Bankhead

There will be sex after death, we just won't be able to feel it.

—Lily Tomlin

Too much of a good thing can be wonderful.

—Mae West

Free love is sometimes love but never freedom.

—Elizabeth Bibesco

Guilt is the price we pay willingly for doing what we are going to do anyway.

—Isabelle Holland

While forbidden fruit is said to taste sweeter, it usually spoils faster.

—Abigail Van Buren

WORK

The best time for planning a book is while you're doing the dishes.

—Agatha Christie

I shall be an autocrat; that's my trade. And the good Lord will forgive me; that's His.

—Catherine the Great

I believe in censorship. After all, I made a fortune out of it.

—Mae West

I have a brain and a uterus, and I use both.
—Congresswoman Patricia Schroeder

They used to photograph Shirley Temple
through gauze. They should photograph me
through linoleum.

—Tallulah Bankhead

You don't manage people; you manage things.
You lead people.

—Admiral Grace Hooper

I do want to get rich but I never want to do what there is to do to get rich.

— Gertrude Stein

If women can sleep their way to the top, how come they aren't there? ... There must be an epidemic of insomnia out there.

— Ellen Goodman

For an actress to be a success she must have the face of Venus, the brains of Minerva, the grace of Terpsichore, the memory of Macaulay, the figure of Juno, and the hide of a rhinoceros.

—Ethel Barrymore

I'm having trouble managing the mansion. What I need is a wife.

—Governor Ella Grasso

Ginger Rogers did everything that Fred Astaire did. She just did it backwards and in high heels.

—variously attributed to Faith Whittlesey, Linda Ellerbee, and Ann Richards

I will make you shorter by a head.

—Queen Elizabeth I

SELF-ESTEEM

Don't be humble. You're not that great.

—Golda Meir

Some of us are becoming the men we wanted to marry.

—Gloria Steinem

What you have become is the price you paid to get what you used to want.

—Mignon McLaughlin

There is glory in a great mistake.

—Nathalia Crane

A woman is like a teabag—only in hot water do you realize how strong she is.

—Nancy Reagan

You grow up the day you have your first real laugh—at yourself.

—Ethel Barrymore

To say something nice about themselves, this is the hardest thing in the world for people to do. They'd rather take their clothes off.

—Nancy Friday

I have often wished I had time to cultivate
modesty. . . . But I am too busy thinking about
myself.

—Dame Edith Sitwell

People who are always making allowances for
themselves soon go bankrupt.

—Mary Pettibone Poole

People are prone to build a statue of the kind of person that it pleases them to be. And few people want to be forced to ask themselves, "What if there is no me like my statue?"

—Zora Neale Hurston

POLITICS

How could I possibly overthrow the government when I can't even keep my dog down?

—Dorothy Parker

In politics, if you want anything said, ask a man; if you want anything done, ask a woman.

—Prime Minister Margaret Thatcher

One of my correspondents has me convinced that the human race would be saved if the world became one huge nudist colony. I keep thinking how much harder it would be to carry concealed weapons.

—Cyra McFadden

Moses dragged us for forty years through the desert to bring us to the one place in the Middle East where there was no oil.

—Golda Meir

They say women talk too much. If you have worked in Congress you know that the filibuster was invented by men.

—Clare Boothe Luce

There are far too many men in politics and not enough elsewhere.

—Hermione Gingold

The reason there are so few female politicians is that it is too much trouble to put makeup on two faces.

—Maureen Murphy

I asked a man in prison once how he happened to be there and he said he had stolen a pair of shoes. I told him if he had stolen a railroad he would be a United States Senator.

—"Mother" Mary Jones

The First Lady is an unpaid public servant
elected by one person—her husband.
—Lady Bird Johnson

Censorship, like charity, should begin at
home; but unlike charity, it should end there.
—Clare Boothe Luce

Why does a slight tax increase cost you two hundred dollars and a substantial tax cut save you thirty cents?

—Peg Bracken

Ninety-eight percent of the adults in this country are decent, hard-working, honest Americans. It's the other lousy two percent that get all the publicity. But then—we elected them.

—Lily Tomlin

The politicians were talking themselves red, white, and blue in the face.

—Clare Boothe Luce

I must say acting was good training for the political life which lay ahead for us.

—Nancy Reagan

AGING

Perhaps one has to be very old before one learns how to be amused rather than shocked.

—Pearl S. Buck

Remember that as a teenager you are at the last stage in your life when you will be happy to hear that the phone is for you.

—Fran Lebowitz

There are no old people nowadays; they are either "wonderful for their age" or dead.

—Mary Pettibone Poole

I used to dread getting older because I thought I would not be able to do all the things I wanted to do, but now that I am older I find that I don't want to do them.

—Nancy, Lady Astor

An archaeologist is the best husband a
woman can have; the older she gets, the more
interested he is in her.

—Agatha Christie

It's not how old you are, but how you are old.

—Marie Dressler

As I grow older, I become more and more of a Marxist—Groucho, that is. When you have lived two-thirds of your life, you know the value of a good joke.

—Karen DeCrow

I believe the true function of age is memory. I'm recording as fast as I can.

—Rita Mae Brown

The hardest years in life are those between ten and seventy.

—Helen Hayes (at age 84)

Old age is like a plane flying through a storm. Once you are aboard there is nothing you can do.

—Golda Meir

Age is something that doesn't matter, unless you are a cheese.

—Billie Burke

Being young is beautiful, but being old is comfortable.

—Marie von Ebner-Eschenbach

How did I git to be a hundred years old? Well, when I moves, I moves slow. When I sits, I sets loose. And when I worries, I goes to sleep.

—Attributed to an old Appalachian mountain woman

Wisdom doesn't automatically come with old age. Nothing does—except wrinkles. It's true, some wines improve with age. But only if the grapes were good in the first place.

—Abigail Van Buren

Old age is life's parody.

—Simone de Beauvoir

THE
GENDER GAP

From birth to age 18 a girl needs good parents. From 18 to 35 she needs good looks. From 35 to 55 she needs a good personality. From 55 on, she needs good cash.

—Sophie Tucker

Show me a woman who doesn't feel guilty and I'll show you a man.

—Erica Jong

The major concrete achievement of the women's movement in the 1970s was the Dutch treat.

—Nora Ephron

People call me a feminist whenever I express sentiments that differentiate me from a doormat or a prostitute.

—Rebecca West

A man has to be called Joe McCarthy to be called ruthless. All a woman has to do is put you on hold.

—Marlo Thomas

Women are repeatedly accused of taking things personally. I cannot see any other honest way of taking them.

—Marya Mannes

I'm just a person trapped inside a woman's body.

—Elaine Boosler

Woman: the peg on which the wit hangs his jest, the preacher his text, the cynic his grouch, and the sinner his justification.

—Helen Rowland

I think being a woman is like being Irish. . . . Everyone says you're important and nice but you take second place all the same.

—Iris Murdoch

If the world were a logical place, men would ride side-saddle.

—Rita Mae Brown

PEARLS

The average, healthy, well-adjusted adult gets up at 7:30 in the morning feeling just plain awful.

—Jean Kerr

Life's a rash, and then there's death and the itching's over.

—Cynthia Kraman

Enemies are so stimulating.
—Katharine Hepburn

I've been on a constant diet for the last two decades. I've lost a total of 789 pounds. By all accounts, I should be hanging from a charm bracelet.

—Erma Bombeck

Women and elephants never forget.

—Dorothy Parker

The cure for anything is salt water—sweat, tears, or the sea.

—Isak Dinesen

Reality is a crutch for people who can't cope with drugs.

—Lily Tomlin

Whenever you see food beautifully arranged on a plate, you know someone's fingers have been all over it.

—Julia Child

Life is something to do when you can't get to sleep.

—Fran Lebowitz

She runs the gamut of emotions from A to B.
—Dorothy Parker,
on an actress' performance

I believe that people would be alive today if there were a death penalty.

—Nancy Reagan

The opposite of talking isn't listening. The opposite of talking is waiting.

—Fran Lebowitz

Unfortunately, sometimes people don't hear you until you scream.

—Stefanie Powers

One reason I don't drink is I want to know when I'm having a good time.

—Nancy, Lady Astor

I base most of my fashion taste on what doesn't itch.

—Gilda Radner

Any God I ever felt in church I brought in with me.

—Alice Walker

He who laughs, lasts.

—Mary Pettibone Poole

No one would remember the Good Samaritan if he only had good intentions. He had money as well.

—Prime Minister Margaret Thatcher

Everybody gets so much information all day long that they lose their common sense.

—Gertrude Stein

Hope is the feeling you have that the feeling you have isn't permanent.

—Jean Kerr

Brevity—the soul of lingerie.

—Dorothy Parker

Sainthood is acceptable only in saints.

—Pamela Hansford Johnson

A long-standing feud between two famous wits, Clare Boothe Luce and Dorothy Parker, was illustrated one evening when both met at the door of a nightclub. Luce motioned Parker through with: "Age before beauty." Parker retorted: "And pearls before swine."

People are more fun than anybody.
—Dorothy Parker

No good deed goes unpunished.

—Clare Boothe Luce

What I love about cooking is that after a hard day, there is something comforting about the fact that if you melt butter and add flour and then hot stock, IT WILL GET THICK! It's a sure thing! It's a sure thing in a world where nothing is sure.

—Nora Ephron

The text of this book was set in Eva Antiqua by
Snap-Haus Graphics, Dumont, New Jersey.

Book design by Diane Stevenson /
Snap-Haus Graphics